Curio:
oi
Berk:

A County Guide
to the Unusual
by
Michael Watson

S.B. Publications

To Joan and Jim Bennett
to mark their Golden Wedding Anniversary.
1946-96

First published in 1996 by S.B. Publications
c/o 19 Grove Road, Seaford, East Sussex BN25 1TP

ISBN 1 85770 109 7

Typeset, printed and bound by MFP Design and Print,
Longford Trading Estate, Thomas Street, Stretford, Manchester M32 0JT

CONTENTS

HUNGERFORD AREA

Front Cover.   Reverse of King James I Coat of Arms, St Michael's Church, Bray
Back Cover.   Wild crocus field at Inkpen
Title Page.   Road signs at Arborfield and Lambourn

WHERE IS THIS MODEL?
(Clue: Look for a silver horse)

By the same author: *Curiosities of Wiltshire*
In preparation: *Curiosities of Bristol*
Curiosities of Somerset

INTRODUCTION

The Royal County of Berkshire has been home to the kings and queens of England for nine centuries. The royal presence has had its effect: here you will find the only blue post box, three major race courses and lions *guardant* everywhere. It is almost impossible to consider the history of the county's people and buildings without finding links with royalty. This nearness seems to have augmented the effects of political events: for example, the destruction of the great abbey of Reading which left the county with no potential cathedral. There has been a need to change with the times - as the Vicar of Bray would agree. Those who kept to the old ways met with disaster and even death in Berkshire. Old industries have been replaced: there is no silk factory in Wokingham - no iron foundry in Bucklebury. The A4, the Bath Road on which 50 stage coaches a day passed through Hungerford, has lost importance to the M4 - on which the county can be crossed from urban east to rural west in 45 minutes. But don't: Royal Berkshire and Berkshire people have much to offer.

Michael Watson

ACKNOWLEDGEMENTS

The photograph on page 2 appears by gracious permission of Her Majesty The Queen.

The photograph on page 6 is reproduced by permission of the British Post Office.

The author thanks all who helped in the preparation of this book and especially those who gave permission for reference to their property:

Lord Howard de Walden, Sir William Benyon DL, Dr Ron Baxter FSA, Gerry Gibbons Esq, Mrs Becky Kennedy, Andrew Plumridge Esq RIBA FRSA and David Simonds Esq,

the incumbents of the many churches featured,

the Director General Equipment Support (Army),

the Headmaster Bradfield College, the Headmaster Shaw House Comprehensive School and the Headteacher Ufton Court Centre,

the Librarians of Newbury, Reading and Windsor Public Libraries,

the Curators of Corinium, Newbury District, REME and Slough Museums and the Curator, The Museum of Reading,

The National Trust, Berkshire Buckinghamshire and Oxfordshire Nature Trust, The Tree Register of the British Isles and The Stanley Spencer Gallery,

The Royal Berkshire Real Tennis Club and Datchet Border Morris,

LEGOLAND Windsor, Monkey Island Hotel, The British Post Office and Wyld Court Rainforest Ltd,

Maidenhead Advertiser, Newbury Weekly News and Slough & Windsor Express.

WINDSOR

KINGS' BEASTS

Access: Within Windsor Castle. Open to the public.

Map reference: Sheet 175 SU968770

From outside the castle wall, strange stone beasts can be seen on the skyline.

St George's Chapel was built between 1475 and 1509 to mark the reconciliation of the dynastic houses of York and Lancaster and the end of the Wars of the Roses. Monarchs over centuries have adopted heraldic animals - real or fabulous - and so the chapel's flying buttresses were crowned by sculptures of the families' beasts: York on the north side, Lancaster on the south. The chapel decayed; in 1682, Sir Christopher Wren removed the heavy beasts to prevent further damage. They were lost. Though repairs were made, the chapel required further attention in the 1920s. Master builder Frederick Minter (1887-1976) contributed the set of 76 beasts seen today. They include the Griffon of Plantagenet King Edward III, the Swan of Lancastrian King Henry V, the Hart of Yorkist King Richard III and the Dragon of Tudor King Henry VII who inherited it from King Cadwaladr of Gwynedd.

But the Yale of the Beauforts must be the strangest: in heraldry, a silver goat with gold spots, it sports both tusks and horns.

WINDSOR

QUEEN MARY'S DOLLS' HOUSE

> *Access:* Within Windsor Castle. Open to the public.
>
> *Map reference:* Sheet 174 SU969769

The Royal Collection © Her Mejesty The Queen

The house was designed by the architect Edwin Lutyens as a present from the nation to Queen Mary, consort of King George V and an avid collector of objets d'art. For nearly three years, its building brought together 1500 craftsmen and artists at a time when many believed that The Great War had dealt British expertise a mortal blow. The house became the centrepiece of the British Empire Exhibition of 1924; it is a time capsule: a comprehensive record of standards of the day on a scale of one inch to the foot.

The library (above) epitomises the architect's intention. The elegantly bound books contain manuscript work by writers of the day, including Kipling, Conan Doyle and the Poet Laureate Robert Bridges. Two chests are filled with minute original pictures: from cartoonists like Heath Robinson, illustrators like Arthur Rackham and portraitists like Rothenstein. Two of King George's favourite pursuits are recognised in the Purdey shot guns and a stamp album compiled by Stanley Gibbons.

Above the library, the King's suite includes a lavishly festooned bed made by the Royal School of Needlework; beneath it stands the royal chamber pot and in the bathroom is his toothbrush - made by Addis from the finest hair available.

The house is full of the products of famous companies: working lifts by Otis, silver by Garrard, china by Wedgwood, pianos by Broadwood, clocks by Cartier, pipes by Dunhill and calendars (for 1924) by WH Smith. Berry Brothers supplied over 60 dozen bottles of wine and spirits, each correctly filled and corked and with facsimile labels - including Chateau Lafite's.

At basement level, the house has garaging for six cars opposite a flower-filled garden set in eternal summer and designed by Lutyens' colleague Gertrude Jekyll. There is a bird on its nest and a snail which has escaped the attention of absentee gardeners who have abandoned their Atco mower.

Indeed, there are no human figures in the house. There is a cat and captive mouse and a yellow parrot but no sign of Queen Mary's six children for whom King George said he made a very good lap. From the Day Nursery, however, a voice has been heard: HMV supplied an exquisite working gramophone with six one-inch diameter records. Five are instrumental but the sixth carries the voice of a baritone singing 'God Save our Gracious King'.

WINDSOR

NELL GWYN'S HOUSE

Access:	From Castle Hill walk 30 yards into Church Street, look left for Number 5.
Map reference:	Sheet 175 SU969769

Eleanor Gwyn (1650-1687) is described in Samuel Pepys diary entry for 3 April 1665 as "pretty and witty". Originally from Hereford, she became a popular comedienne in London's bawdy Restoration theatre. Pepys reported that King Charles II saw her perform on 2 March 1667 shortly before there were strained relations between the monarch and his mistress, Lady Castlemaine. Pepys was not alone in lusting after the teenager - "the King did send several times for Nelly." In later entries, the jealous Pepys describes Nell Gwyn as "that jade" and "a bold merry slut". In 1670 she bore the king a son, Charles Beauclerk, who was created Duke of St Albans in 1684. He became Lord Lieutenant of Berkshire.

Nell's house in Windsor is uncharacteristically strait and narrow.

WINDSOR

A LEANING HOUSE

Windsor is famous for its buildings but not all are elegantly upright Georgian essays. It is difficult to avoid the word 'quaint' on seeing Market Cross House.

Next door, stands the sturdy Guildhall of 1689. Sir Christopher Wren completed the project after the death of its designer Sir Thomas Fitch. Supporting the council chamber was a double row of pillars. Anxious councillors, certain that the floor would collapse, ordered Wren to erect a central row; he did so under protest - but to prove that his engineering was sound, he left a small gap between each pillar and the underside of the chamber.

WINDSOR

A SPECIAL POST BOX

> *Access:* From Castle Hill, turn left into High Street and walk 200 yards to the junction with St Albans Street.
>
> *Map reference:* Sheet 175 SU969767

Royal Mail boxes have been painted bright red since 1884 - this one is blue.

To mark the coronation of King George V in 1911, an air mail link was set up between this pillar box and Hendon in North London - a distance of 19 miles.

A Blériot XI monoplane (below) piloted by Gustave Hamel inaugurated the service which operated from 9-26 September. In that time over 110,000 items were carried. Although an aircraft in India carried mail for 5 miles as part of an exhibition on 18 February 1911, the Post Office can claim to be the first to introduce a regular airmail service.

On 25 July 1909 a Blériot aircraft of the same mark, piloted by its maker, was the first to fly across the English Channel.

© The British Post Office

WINDSOR

TOWER BRIDGE

Access:	From Windsor follow brown signs to LEGOLAND on the B3022.
Map reference:	Sheet 175 SU942746

© LEGOLAND Windsor

This Tower Bridge is in Miniland among the many fascinating attractions of LEGOLAND Windsor, a quarter square mile theme park. A hundred model designers worked for two and a half years - using 20 million LEGO bricks - to create the 800 buildings and 700 other models of Miniland. The landscape architects have even used real miniature trees with miniature leaves here.

The LEGO Group was founded in Denmark - the name comes from the Danish words *leg godt* (play well). Ole Kirk Christianssen, a village carpenter, started by making wooden toys in the 1930s; his son introduced the plastic building bricks now available in 134 countries.

Tower Bridge was built by Henrik Lykke - a fitting tribute to the century-old original.

ETON

A RARE PILLAR BOX

Access:	From Windsor's Castle Hill walk down Thames Street, cross Windsor Bridge into High Street Eton. Box is beside The Cockpit (No 47) on the right.
Map reference:	Sheet 175 SU967774

In 1856 the Post Office ordered a new design for a pillar box in the form of a fluted column with a vertical aperture surmounted by a dome, cushion and crown. Due to a misunderstanding by the manufacturers, the pillar boxes measured 8 feet (2.4m) high! Later the same year an amended design replaced the dome and crown with a flattened cone, as shown above. In 1857 the box was redesigned with a horizontal aperture, with four examples still in use today.

The vertical slot is intended to deter thieves. The snag is that - despite the flap - the design makes it easier for the rain to get in. Eton's rare pillar box is one of ten in existence; eight of which are still in use today.

The oldest pillar box still in use on the British mainland stands at Barnes Cross, near Sherborne, Dorset. The pillar box was made in 1853.

DATCHET

MORRIS MEN

Access:	Dances may be seen at summer carnivals and fetes in the area. Tourist Information Offices have details.

© Datchet Border Morris

It may seem odd that Datchet's Morris dancers don't dress in white. This is a Border Morris group whose ancient dances are characteristic of the Welsh Marches. Some researchers say that the word 'Morris' is a corruption of 'Morisque' which refers to the Moors - hence the blacked faces. The tradition was recorded in the 15th century at about the time the Christians overcame the Moorish Empire in Europe - which might explain the combative nature of the dance. Other researchers suggest that Morris dancing has roots in Indo-European fertility rites and point to the animal-man references. Whatever the origins of this colourful centuries-old tradition, it is believed to bring good fortune to its spectators.

OLD WINDSOR

MAGNA CARTA

Access:	From Windsor take A308 south-east for 3 miles through Old Windsor to Runnymede meadows. (NT). NB: The island is private property.
Map reference:	Sheet 175 SU997732

In 1209, King John was excommunicated after a dispute with the Pope; the interdict imposed on England prevented Mass being said for six years. The resulting popular disquiet combined with the effects of punitive taxation and economic inflation led to widespread rebellion. When the French threatened invasion, the King accepted the supremacy of the Pope and with fresh support attacked them. But the King's ignominious defeat in July 1214 made matters worse. In May 1215, rebels captured London. Leaders of the English peerage set out conditions for John to remain King. He agreed to meet the barons on neutral ground midway between his fortress at Windsor and the rebel encampment at Staines in Surrey.

The island of Runnymede was an ancient meeting place: its name comes from *runinge* - 'to take council'. King John signed the Magna Carta here to buy time; in this he failed: England was wracked again by civil war. However, the powerful language had a life of its own: it became the model for numerous charters of rights. This place has special meaning for citizens of the United States whose constitution is based on Magna Carta.

OLD WINDSOR

EMLYN'S ORDER

Access: From Windsor take A309 3¹/₂ miles towards Staines. Turn right onto A328, first right and park. Walk into Beaumont business park, go straight ahead and circle buildings clockwise to reach lawns in front of the projecting porch of original white lodge.

Map reference: Sheet 175 SU990732

The Society of Jesus bought the estate in 1854 and founded Beaumont College here. The lodge had been built in 1790 by local architect Henry Emlyn (1729-1815). He thought it time that there was an English order of column to supplement the Roman Palladian styles which dominated; he published his ideas in 1781 but they were greeted without enthusiasm. Probably the only extant example is seen here: coupled columns grow from a common lower section with a Garter Star cartouche (inspired by his work on St George's Chapel) to decorate the junction "rather like a figleaf" - as Sir John Betjeman put it. The capital is especially awkward and seems to have resulted from much redrafting. Soon afterwards, the "primitive power" of early Greek orders came into fashion.

SUNNINGDALE

A ROMAN TEMPLE

Access:	From Windsor take A322 south 3 miles through the Park, bear left onto B383. After 2 miles, turn left into Mill Lane for 1 mile to A329. Turn left, go ¼ mile to Blacknest car park. In Park, walk east beside lake for 1 mile. Ruins are on right.
Map reference:	Sheet 175 SU975687

In 1816, the Bey of Tripoli in Libya presented the 'Bey' of England - the Prince Regent - with a majestic ruin. Leptis Magna was a Phoenician port. After nearby Carthage was razed by the Romans in 146BC, Leptis prospered; it became a Roman colonia in the reign of Emperor Trajan (98-117AD). Emperor Severus (193-211) was born in Leptis and many public buildings like this temple were in Severan style. But Leptis declined; it became an exorchate of Christian Byzantium and was destroyed by the Moslem Arabs in 697. The temple was despatched with difficulty to London and stored for six years until, in 1826, the Royal Engineers erected it as a folly beside Virginia Water.

SUNNINGHILL

THE RANEE'S CINEMA

<table>
<tr><td>Access:</td><td>From Windsor take A322 through Windsor Great Park to double roundabout junction with A330. Go left on A330 (Winkfield Road) a mile to A30, turn left. After a mile, turn right into Sunninghill Road. Novello Theatre is 600 yards on left opposite school.</td></tr>
<tr><td>Map reference:</td><td>Sheet 175 SU936678</td></tr>
</table>

James Brooke (1803-1868) went to Sarawak in 1840 to combat piracy and headhunting for the Malay ruler who was heir to the Sultan of Brunei. Brooke's reward, appointment as governor in 1841, began the rule of the White Rajahs which continued until 1946. The second Rajah's wife, Ranee Margaret, was an accomplished pianist from Wiltshire. While living at Grey Friars, she provided the local people with a 300-seat village cinema in which she accompanied silent films. The cinema continued in business until 1986 when it succumbed to competition. But the building survived to become the 160-seat children's Novello Theatre. How many of today's audience know that it exists because a Victorian adventurer vanquished pirates 8000 miles away?

ASCOT

HATS VERSUS HORSES

Access:	From Windsor take A322 through Windsor Great Park to Ascot. On race days, follow signs to car park.
Map reference:	Sheet 175 SU922688

© Slough & Windsor Express

Ascot racecourse was built in 1711 by Queen Anne's Master of the Buckhounds, the Duke of Somerset. King George II's son, the Duke of Cumberland - whose horses were trained at East Ilsley - became patron in 1744 (a year before he distinguished himself at the Battle of Culloden). The close royal connection was enhanced by the Prince Regent, the future King George IV. During his reign, in 1825, the first formal Royal Drive was held. Originally a procession of noblemen displaying the magnificent carriages prepared for the King's Levee, it is now a high point of the June week of racing: Royal Ascot. Gold Cup Day, the Thursday, soon became known as Ladies' Day - when milliners' creativity competes with the racing for attention.

SLOUGH

CELESTIAL DISCOVERIES

Access: From Windsor take A355 to Slough. At A4 (Bath Road) turn right then right again into Montem Road. Park at Leisure Centre. Walk back to Bath Road, turn right 200 yards to Slough Museum.

Map reference: Sheet 175 SU967801

In 1781, Frederick William Herschel (1738-1822) discovered Uranus - the first new planet to be found since prehistoric times. German-born, he came to England as a musician and developed expertise in grinding lenses before taking up astronomy. In 1782 he was appointed the private astronomer to King George III. Having settled in Slough at Observatory House in 1786, he built the biggest telescope of his day - a 40 foot long reflector - in his garden. He was able to say: "I have looked further into space than ever human being did before me." His son John, born in Slough in 1792, became a leading mathematician. He continued his father's work on the Milky Way, galaxies and nebulae and later pioneered the use of photography in astronomy. Slough Museum has a scale model of the great telescope which once stood in the town - a place more often associated with the edible versions of the Herschels' objects of interest.

SLOUGH
CAUGHT BY LINE

Access: From Windsor take A355 to Slough. At A4 (Bath Road) turn right, then
right again into Montem Road. Park at Leisure Centre. Walk back to
Bath Road, turn right 200 yards to Slough Museum.

Map reference: Sheet 175 SU969800

On New Year's Day 1845, John Tawell poisoned his former mistress in Salt Hill. He fled to the station and caught an evening train to London. But his victim's screams had been heard by someone able to describe him to the police. A message was passed over the Great Western Railway telegraph line to Paddington. When the unsuspecting murderer arrived, he was followed home by plain clothes officers. In due course, he was hanged.

Slough's telegraph was installed in 1843 as an integral part of the railway. On 6 August 1844 it was used to send news of the birth of Queen Victoria's second son at Windsor Castle to her ministers in London. Two months after the station opened in June 1840, the Dowager Queen Adelaide, widow of King William IV, became the first royal personage to travel by train.

HOLYPORT

A ROYAL GAME

Access:	From Windsor, take A308 2½ miles towards Maidenhead. Before motorway bridge, turn left to Holyport ¾ mile. Bear right at green to the Belgian Arms. Entrance to Royal Berkshire Real Tennis Club is 50 yards further and down private road. NB: Spectators are admitted at the manager's discretion.
Map reference:	Sheet 175 SU891779

Real Tennis is a medieval game once played (and gambled upon) by the young King Henry VIII. The court's design and the game's rules are complex: four irregularly sized walls, three with roofs border an area bisected by a sagging net. The game is played with pear-shaped racquets and hard cloth balls. The scoring system was inherited by the modern game of lawn tennis. One part of the floor near the net is the 'hazard court'. The word 'hazard' came from the name of a French dice-game of chance which gained it from Spanish when the Moors ruled half the country. *Az-zahr* is Arabic for 'the chance'.

BRAY

SURVIVORS

Access:	From Windsor, take A308 2½ miles towards Maidenhead. Turn right into Upper Bray Road 1½ mile to High Street. After The Hinds Head turn right for St Michaels Church.
Map reference:	Sheet 175 SU902797

King James I ordered the Established Church to display the arms of the Crown. The Stuart arms introduced a Scottish unicorn supporter in place of the Tudor dragon; the Scottish red lion (gold here) and Irish harp were quartered with King Edward III's fleur-de-lys and Norman lions on the shield. Erected in 1604, the arms on the screen of the south aisle are double-sided (the reverse side is shown on the front cover) This unusual version survived Cromwell's Commonwealth because it was hidden.

A song of 1734 tells of a high church man in good King Charles's golden days (when loyalty no harm meant) who preached that "Kings are by God appointed". He swore that "whatsoever King may reign, I will be Vicar of Bray" - and was despite the varied religious leanings of successive rulers. The vicar's name is unknown. Did he, as the song suggests, serve Bray for (say) the 45 years between 1647 - King Charles I's time - and 1692 (after the arms had been hidden and retrieved and Protestant King William III replaced Catholic King James II)? Did an earlier version of the song refer to King Henry's golden days and the Reformation between 1525 and 1570? Records of imcumbents are incomplete but research continues. Few churches have been made so famous by a song.

BRAY

MONKEY BUSINESS

Access: From Windsor, take A308 2½ miles towards Maidenhead. Turn right into Upper Bray Road ½ mile to High Street. Follow signs for Monkey Island Hotel. The Monkey Room is in the Restaurant Pavilion, left over the foot bridge.

Map reference: Sheet 175 SU914791

The Rococo phase in Baroque art put informality and fun into the design of the minor royal buildings of early 18th century France. Paintings of monkeys in human situations - *singerie* - became popular. In the 1720s Charles Spencer built this fishing lodge on Monk's Eyot (Monkey Island) in the Thames. In 1733 he inherited the Dukedom of Marlborough from his Aunt Henrietta and had to curb his rakish ways. The ceiling of the lodge's octagonal parlour was decorated by de Clermont in the manner of Charles III Audran, master of *singerie* and tutor of Watteau. It must have provided comic relief from the grandeur of Blenheim Palace.

MAIDENHEAD
A DARING DESIGN

Access:	From Windsor, take A355 north to M4 J6 westbound. Leave at J7. At A4 go left for 2 miles. Turn left into River Road. Walk the footpath to bridge.
Map reference:	Sheet 175 SU902810

Isambard Kingdom Brunel's Great Western Railway bridge has the longest, flattest brick arches in the world. When work began in 1837, people scoffed at the design and predicted failure. But when a gale destroyed the scaffolding in 1839, the structure stood firm; the only sign of distortion is in the eastern arch where centering was removed before the mortar was set. The bridge's completion allowed the railway to link London and Bristol in 1841; it is still used frequently by trains of the Great Western.

In 1844 the bridge was depicted by JMW Turner in his painting Rain, Steam and Speed.

COOKHAM

SIR STANLEY'S PRAM

Access: From Windsor take A308 5¹/₂ miles to Maidenhead junction with A4. Turn right on A4 for 1 mile, turn left onto A4094. Go 2¹/₂ miles to Cookham. Stanley Spencer Gallery is on junction with High Street.

Map reference: Sheet 175 SU897853

Born and bred in Cookham, the painter Stanley Spencer (1891-1959) has been hailed as the successor of Blake and the Pre-Raphaelites. His early work was much influenced by his experiences of war in the Salonica campaign of 1916-18. Later, he used Cookham's everyday people and places in large scale works - his 'Resurrection' of 1927 is set in the village churchyard. His mode of working and unworldly attitude to his finances gave this battered pram an essential role in his life.

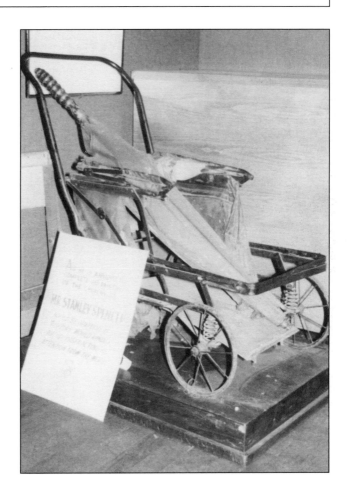

COOKHAM

THE TARRY STONE

Access:	From Windsor take A308 5¹/₂ miles to Maidenhead junction with A4. Turn right on A4 for 1 mile, turn left onto A4094. Go 2¹/₂ miles to Cookham. Stone is on junction with lane to Odney.
Map reference:	Sheet 175 SU897854

This sarsen boulder once marked the boundary of the Abbot of Cirencester's land holding - the abbey ruins are more than a stone's throw away in Gloucestershire: 55 miles. In addition to becoming a focus for games and festivals - Stanley Spencer included it in a painting - the Tarry Stone is a traditional tryst for courting couples. Originally in the High Street closer to the moor, it is now on a more suitable site for those tarrying.

COOKHAM

SWAN UPPING

Access: From Windsor take A308 5¹/₂ miles to Maidenhead junction with A4.
Turn right on A4 for 1 mile, turn left onto A4094. Go 2¹/₂ miles to
Cookham Bridge.

Map reference: Sheet 175 SU897856

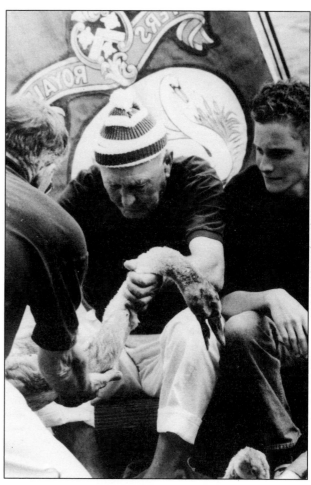

© Maidenhead Advertiser

In the time of King Henry III, swan meat was considered such a rare delicacy that only the king could authorise its consumption: swans belonged automatically to the Crown. Later, the City of London's livery companies were permitted to own swans on the Thames. So as to recognise their property, each marked its birds' beaks with its own pattern. Today, only the Dyers and Vintners own swans which are not the Queen's. In July, under the auspices of the Queen's Swan Keeper - an office introduced by King Edward III - young swans are upped from the water and marked: one nick for the Dyers - two for the Vintners. Those unmarked belong to Her Majesty.

BISHAM

AN ABBOT'S CURSE

Access:	From Windsor go north on A355 to M4 J6. Go west 5 miles to J8/9 and take A404M to J9b. Follow A404M and A404 for 6 miles. Turn left for village. ³/₄mile later on sharp right bend, go straight on to church.
Map reference:	Sheet 175 SU848854

The Knights Templar, founded in Jerusalem in 1118, built a college at Bisham. It became an Augustinian priory after the Templars were suppressed for heresy in 1307. In 1537, it became a Benedictine abbey which was dissolved only three years later. The lands were granted first to Anne of Cleves - whom King Henry VIII married that year - and then, in 1553, Catholic Queen Mary I granted it to Sir Thomas Hoby who had been suspected of plotting against her Protestant father. But the abbot had cursed Bisham vowing that the estate would never pass directly to a male heir. Sir Thomas's wife Elizabeth, whose effigy graces All Saints Church, is reputed to have killed her eldest son. The abbey - now the home of The Sports Council - is believed to be haunted by her remorseful ghost.

HURLEY

MEAT FOR MONKS

Access: From Windsor go north on A355 to M4 J6. Go west 5 miles to J8/9 and take A404M to J9b. Follow A404M and A404 for 3 miles to slip road to A4130 towards Henley. A mile later, turn right to Hurley. Walk past Tithe Barn towards river. Dovecote is seen through a gateway on left. NB: Private property.

Map reference: Sheet 175 SU825841

Hurley Priory existed before the Domesday Book was compiled in 1086; remains of its buildings are scattered about the village - typical of the havoc wreaked by King Henry VIII's commissioners. A splendid Tudor mansion stands on the site of the infirmary; the priory's guest house - dating from 1187 - is now The Olde Bell Hotel. A survivor after six centuries is the monks' massive dovecote, source of fresh meat and an indicator of the high standard of living enjoyed by the Benedictine community.

LITTLEWICK GREEN
A CORNER OF RURITANIA

> *Access:* From Windsor go north on A355 to M4 J6. Go west 5 miles to J8/9 and
> take A404M to J9b. Go left on A4 1¼ miles, go left into village.
> Redroofs is the last building before the village school.
>
> *Map reference:* Sheet 175 SU840799

The village green - complete with pub and cricket - seems an unlikely setting for
Ruritanian fantasy, yet in 1947 actor-composer Ivor Novello was inspired to write
King's Rhapsody here.

In 1927, at the height of his career as a silent film hearthrob, Novello was
determined to buy the rather expensive Munro Lodge. That year Noel Coward had
been chosen instead of him to play the lead in the stage version of the best-selling
novel *The Constant Nymph*. Huffily, Novello refused the role in the film version but
the producer was persistent: the actor was paid what he asked - enough to buy the
house which he renamed Redroofs. In this quiet corner, he wrote a "lovely part for
myself" as an ageing prince who loves a young actress. He died on 6 March 1951
hours after performing to an ecstatic audience which he had lifted for an evening
from the austerity of post-war England. His funeral attracted huge crowds and the
ceremony was broadcast on radio.

Redroofs, to which came Greta Garbo, Cary Grant and Noel Coward, is now a
theatre school: a living memorial to a much-loved entertainer.

READING

AN UNBALANCED LION

Access:	In Forbury Gardens.
Map reference:	Sheet 175 SU725737

In April 1880, Afghan troops mutinied against Wali Sher Ali Khamis who asked for British help. Brigadier Burrowes' brigade was sent but on 27 July he was outnumbered twelve to one near Maiwand; his withdrawal became a bloody rout in which he lost 1000 men of whom 285 were of Berkshire's 66th Regiment. In August, Kandahar was beseiged by the Russian-backed rebels. General Roberts - who was to become a hero of the Boer War - was sent post-haste to relieve the city. He succeeded but within a few months politicians had decided to abandon the plan to expand British influence in the region. The soldiers were withdrawn.

The Maiwand Lion was sculpted by George Simmonds of the local brewing family and erected in 1884 to commemorate the fallen. Unlike the heraldic Lion Passant Guardant, the Maiwand Lion is in a state of imbalance: Simmonds' critics observed that if the beast tried to step forward it would fall over. Perhaps its stance is an unconscious comment on the politicians who sent so many to futile death.

Among the 66th's wounded was Surgeon-Major Preston whose experiences Conan Doyle gave to Sherlock Holmes' companion, Dr Watson.

READING

A ROYAL FOUNDATION

Access:	Follow town walk signs to the abbey ruins. The plaque is on the north wall.
Map reference:	Sheet 175 SU726737

King Henry I, fourth son of William the Conqueror, died in Normandy in December 1135 having reigned for 35 years. Despite lengthy absences from England, he did much to integrate the Normans with local people - bringing peace and the rule of law. He founded Reading Abbey in 1121 by installing a handful of monks from Cluny in Burgundy - men who followed St Benedict's rule and who became champions of Romanesque art. It was to the incomplete church that King Henry's body was brought for burial. By the time the church was consecrated by Thomas à Becket on 19 April 1164, it was richly endowed: it owned the town of Reading together with extensive parkland and outlying manors. King Henry's daughter Matilda, widow of the Holy Roman Emperor, gave the hand of St James as its chief relic - this and a piece of the true cross ensured a steady flow of pilgrims with money to spend. The abbot was granted a fair on the feast of St

Laurence and authority to strike coin. Sadly, the King's generosity led to friction between the abbey and town which culminated in the gleeful destruction of King Henry I's magnificent foundation in the reign of his descendant King Henry VIII thirteen generations later.

A reminder of the origin of the Normans may be seen in The Museum of Reading's reconstruction of part of the abbey's Romanesque cloister which was built around 1125. It features the earliest surviving example in England of the 'beakhead' motif found also at Avington (below). Scholars see English Romanesque as a melding of pagan Norse energy, Anglo-Saxon characteristics and European style; this form is peculiarly English. The beak gripping a roll of masonry is reminiscent of the 'gripping beasts' found in 9th century Norse art wherein Fenrir the wolf-son of Loki, catalyst of evil, is locked in combat with Odin the All-Father. Or perhaps the beaks were of ravens, the familiars of Odin whom pagan Saxons called Woden. The Norman Conquest of England came only 154 years after the Norse war-lord Ganger-Rolf (or Rollo) embraced Christianity and was granted extensive lands in northern France where he established the Norse - or Northman - Duchy of Normandy. The present Duke is Her Majesty the Queen.

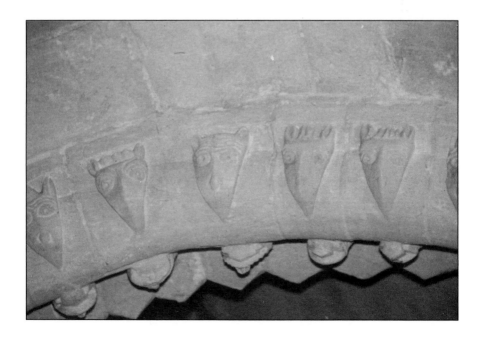

READING

SPRING SONG

Access: Follow town walk signs to the abbey ruins. Go to the chapter house.

Map reference: Sheet 175 SU726736

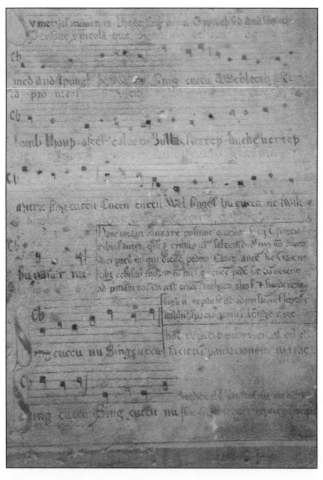

On the north wall of the ruined chapter house of Reading Abbey is a plaque inscribed with the words and music of *Sumer is icumen in,* a 750-year old English language pop song, the earliest of its type in the world. It was found written in a record book in what scholars believe to be the hand of John of Fornsete, a monk appointed Keeper of the Cartulary - the abbey records - in the early 13th century. The composition is in the form of a six-part canon and, unlike sacred music of the period, is written - not in one of the old modes associated with plainsong - but in the modern key of F. Benjamin Britten quotes the song in his 1949 work, *Spring Symphony.*

You can listen to the song in its original form at The Museum of Reading.

READING

PUNISHMENT

Access:	From Forbury Gardens, follow signs to abbey ruins. Follow prison wall to open area.
Map reference:	Sheet 175 SU726735

King Henry VIII's Dissolution of the Monasteries Act of 1536 was aimed at lesser houses but it was opposed vigorously by powerful clerics like Hugh of Faringdon, Abbot of Reading. The rebellion known as The Pilgrimage of Grace followed. Although the king promised the rebels pardon if they surrendered, 200 were charged with high treason. In 1539, Abbot Hugh was hanged, drawn and quartered within sight of his abbey which was then despoiled. The valuable Caen stone was plundered leaving only the flint rubble core to be seen today.

Reading gaol, completed in 1844, stands on the site of the chancel where King Henry I was buried in 1136. Designed by the young Gilbert Scott who was to become the architect of the Albert Memorial in London, the gaol was made famous by Oscar Wilde who, while serving two years hard labour, wrote *The Ballad of Reading Gaol*. He was inspired by the fate of a fellow prisoner, Charles Woolridge, who was hanged on 7 July 1896 for cutting the throat of his unfaithful wife Laura.

> *For Man's grim Justice goes its way*
> *And will not swerve aside:*
> *It slays the weak, it slays the strong,*
> *It has a deadly stride ...*

The words seem a fitting comment on the fate of the abbey and its last abbot.

READING
BLOWN AWAY

Access: In St Laurence churchyard close to the east gate.

Map reference: Sheet 174 SU717736

When, in 1839, the Great Western Railway's directors rejected Brunel's plans for a single-sided station for Reading, Brunel responded by substituting a design which was described as "cheap and ugly". As a result of this delay and the wet winter of 1839/40, time was short. Work continued on the station after the directors first travelled the line on 14 March 1840. On 24 March, a freak whirlwind removed several tons of the roof and dislodged Henry West, a glazier who was working on it. Henry's memorial is a railing which has been renewed from time to time. Brunel's station, which was opened to the public six days after Henry's death, was rebuilt in 1899.

St Laurence's was built in the early 12th century to replace a Saxon church demolished during the construction of Reading Abbey. On the south side of the present church once stood the public entrance - the Compter Gate - of the abbey.

READING

REGULAR FIGURES

Access:	In St Laurence's Church, on the south wall. NB: Access may be possible only at the times of services.
Map reference:	Sheet 175 SU723736

Mathematician John Blagrave, who died in 1611, studied at St Johns College Oxford which was founded by Sir Thomas White of Reading in 1555. He is commemorated by a monument which includes five regular solid figures borne by bare-breasted young ladies. One wonders if the author of *The Mathematical Jewel* was unduly fond of ladies: in his will he left instructions that every year a maid servant from each of the three parishes who had completed five years service with one master should cast lots for a prize of 15 sovereigns - one for each maid-year of service.

Another Reading man who studied at St Johns was William Laud, Archbishop of Canterbury. He was baptised in St Laurence's in 1573. After King Charles I appointed him to write a prayer book for use by both the English and Scots, the latter formed the Covenanter Army and fought the Bishops' War. Laud was impeached as an evil counsellor and beheaded in 1645.

John Blagrave's nephew Daniel, a lawyer and MP, was one of 67 commissioners at the trial of King Charles I; his signature is on the king's death warrant. The king was beheaded on 30 January 1649. At the Restoration in 1660, the regicide Blagrave fled to Germany; he died in Aachen in 1668.

READING
BOWDLERISED BAYEUX

Access: In the Museum of Reading in Blagrave Street, next to the Town Hall.

Map reference: Sheet 174 SU723737

The world's only full sized replica of the Bayeux Tapestry - which, in fact, is embroidery - was made in 1885-6 in Leek, Staffordshire by a group of 35 ladies. In 1895, after a long exhibition tour, the 70-metre long fabric came to Reading where it was bought for the town by a former mayor, Alderman Arthur Hill. The ladies were faithful to the original in design, materials and stitching - but there is one difference. The original of the mysterious Aelfgyva and Cleric scene's border depicts a full-frontally exposed naked man (below); Margaret J.Ritchie of the Leek Embroidery Society gave him shorts.

READING

NUNHIDE TOWER

Access: Take A4 west for 4 miles past Calcot to roundabout before M4. Turn right then left and left again onto lane skirting motorway. 50 yards before Nunhide Farm park and walk footpath to tower.

Map reference: Sheet 175 SU649725

Possibly the most frequently seen folly in England, little is known about this tower of local brick. Folly experts date it to about 1830 and think it once had an external wooden staircase to give access to a top floor. Old maps describe it as a dovecote but it is a long way from a large kitchen. It might have been built as an observation point over hunting country now bisected by the M4; similar follies have been built as eyecatchers in the landscaped parkland of a grand house - Sulham perhaps. It is now surrounded by a golf course.

TIDMARSH

AN ODD APSE

Access: From Reading take A4 5¹/₂ miles west to A340 roundabout. Go right towards Pangbourne for 3¹/₄ miles. Church is on right side of road.

Map reference: Sheet 174 SU635746

The octagonal plan of the apse is a feature found more often in French than English churches. St Laurence's is said to date from about 1220, perhaps half a century after the nave was built. However, a similar apse in Wing, Buckinghamshire, takes its shape from a Saxon 8th century crypt beneath the chancel. Perhaps Tidmarsh - whose name has a Saxon origin - has a church of similar antiquity.

The decoration of the Norman south door includes chevrons with a distinctly beaky look. The impression given is that they were an early derivative of the beakhead motif found at Avington (SU372679).

BRADFIELD

GREEK THEATRE

Access:	From Reading take A4 5½ miles west to A340 roundabout. Go right towards Pangbourne ¼ mile, turn left go 2 miles to Bradfield. At crossroads turn right. Theatre is 100 yards on left. NB: Open only when plays are performed publicly.
Map reference:	Sheet 175 SU605727

In 1880, dynamic Dr H.B.Gray became headmaster of Bradfield College, a school with a strong classics tradition. Ten years later, aided by sixth formers and advised by the College Engineer E.Foulke, he built a 1600 seater theatre in a nearby chalk pit. He modelled it on the 4th century BC Greek amphitheatre at Epidauros. It may not be surrounded by thyme-scented olive groves, but the trees around Dr Gray's theatre give it a special aura. The first play performed was Sophocles' tragedy Antigone. The theatre is in frequent use and triennially for over a century, the college has presented a classic play to the public.

PANGBOURNE

A GOOD SUBSTANTIAL BRIDGE

Access:	From Reading take the A329 Oxford road 6¹/₂ miles to Pangbourne. Turn right onto B471, go 300 yards to car park on right. Toll house is on opposite bank of river.
Map reference:	Sheet 175 SU636768

By Act of Parliament, Whitchurch Bridge over the Thames is extra-parochial - not subject to the rule of either Berkshire or Oxfordshire. The original bridge of 1792, which replaced a ferry, was narrow and had steep ramps. No doubt many a mule driver thought 2¹/₂ old pennies a lot to pay for the privilege of dragging an obstinate animal up the slope. The second bridge - of 1852 - was more user-friendly. The present iron bridge of 1902 is both elegant and practical. The original toll house still stands though its function has been taken over by modern equipment. The bridge is one of the few which have always been privately owned.

UPPER BASILDON

AN ARCHITECTURAL FISH

<table>
<tr><td>Access:</td><td>From Reading, take Oxford road A329 6½ miles to Pangbourne. At T-junction, turn left onto A340 towards Theale and after 100 yards, right past church 2¼ miles to Upper Basildon. St Stephens Church is on the right.</td></tr>
<tr><td>Map reference:</td><td>Sheet 174 SU 601760</td></tr>
</table>

The church was built with the help of Lord Iliffe of Basildon Park in 1964. The architect, PN Perkins, used the ancient Christian symbol of the fish as a model. Originally a Jewish symbol, the fish was adopted by 2nd century Christians possibly because the Greek acrostic (transliterated) Iesus CHristos, THeou (h)Yios, Soter (Jesus Christ, Son of God, Saviour) produces the word ICHTHYS - a fish.

BASILDON

SUPER SHELL

Access:	From Reading, take Oxford road A329 to Pangbourne. Go on 2 miles to Basildon Park on left of road. (NT)
Map reference:	Sheet 175 SU613785

Like several houses in the area, Basildon Park had connections with the dubious nabobs of the Raj. Clive of India considered buying the old manor house on his return to England in 1767 but it went instead to Sir Francis Sykes, the self-made Resident to the Nawab of Bengal and friend of the Governor General of India, Warren Hastings. In 1772, during the rebuilding of the house by John Carr - architect of Harewood House - the government ordered an enquiry into corruption in India. The committee resolved that functionaries in Bengal had misused the powers of the State for their own enrichment. Clive, who was implicated, killed himself in 1774. Sir Francis was later fined heavily. His family declined; the house passed to others until, stripped of most of its features, the shell faced demolition. It was saved by the 2nd Lord Iliffe, the newspaper publisher, and his wife who energetically collected examples of Carr's work, furniture and paintings, supervised repairs and - when all was returned to a condition that Sykes would have envied - gave Basildon Park to the National Trust.

Lord Iliffe's mother, Lady Charlotte, travelled widely with her husband. A private person, while he concentrated on business, she wandered the beaches and bazaars in search of seashells. The result - probably the finest private collection on show - is housed in The Shell Room. This includes (right) a mid-19th century 'Sailor's Valentine' from Barbados in a style much-copied in later years. There are Japanese Thorny Oysters, Turbans with brilliant trap-door-like cat's-eye to close the molluscs' perculum, incredibly fragile Pen Shells from the Pacific and the rare Spindle Tibia from Taiwan. A

chambered nautilus (below) has been bisected to reveal a structure which is so perfectly regular that it might seem man-made. Some shells have been carved into intricate designs: there are Helmet Shells which were used by Victorians to make cameo portraits for brooches. Around the walls are shell panels designed by Gordon Davies in 1979 and reminiscent of the lost 18th century shell grotto for which Basildon was once famous.

BASILDON

JETHRO TULL, INVENTOR AND MUSICIAN

Access:	From Reading, take Oxford road A329 to Pangbourne. Go on 2 miles, pass Basildon Park, turn right. Cross railway go ¼ mile to car-park.
Map reference:	Sheet 175 SU612793

Against a buttress of the south wall of St Bartholomew's church is a memorial to this pioneer of modern agriculture who invented the seed drill in 1701. He was buried here in 1741. Born in Basildon in 1674, educated as a lawyer and musician, he had to take over his father's estates when only 25. Though his revolutionary methods upset local people, his book on husbandry became famous; it was translated into French and used by Voltaire on his estate.

Nearby is the striking memorial by William Storey to Harold and Ernest Deverell, teenagers drowned in the Thames in 1886. They are depicted in their trunks, contemplating the depths which proved lethal.

HURST

THE LODDON LILY

Access: From Reading, take A329 east to Winnersh. At crossroad with B3030, turn left, go 1½ miles to Hurst. Follow brown signs for Dinton Pastures Country Park. NB: To see the lily, a permit must be obtained from the BBONT office at Dinton.

Map reference: Sheet 175 SU785718

This rare wetland plant flowers in April-May in a reserve on the banks of the River Loddon. The 2-foot high Loddon Lily - *leucojum aestivum,* known incongruously as the Summer Snowflake - came from Central Europe. Its fruits have float chambers which allow it to spread via flood water.

In St Nicholas Church in Hurst village (SU794730), there is an hourglass holder beside the painted Jacobean pulpit. Dated 1636, it incorporates oak leaves signifying the village name - which means 'a wooded hill'. Parishioners unable to concentrate on the sermon might consider the motto facing them: "As this glasse runneth so man's life passethe."

REMENHAM

A MULTINATIONAL BRIDGE

Access: From Reading, take A4 east for 5¹/₂ miles to A321 roundabout. Turn left towards Henley. After 2 miles, at narrow bridge sign, look for private road on right. Bridge is best seen from below.

Map reference: Sheet 175 SU777814

In 1751, Park Place became the residence of Henry Conway (1721-1795), a cousin of the "arbiter of taste" and champion of the light-hearted Gothick style Horace Walpole (1717-1797). Over the years, Conway - an MP who rose to become a Field Marshal and Governor of Jersey (his portrait by Gainsborough is in the Royal Court, St Helier) - played host to a number of follies. This one, sometimes called the Cyclopic Bridge, is built of boulders from 14 countries. The grotto-like structure was built in 1763 by gentleman-architect Thomas Pitt so sturdily that it can take the A321's heavy traffic.

In the private grounds of nearby Temple Combe stand megaliths from the neolithic tomb chamber found on St Helier's Mont de la Ville - the site of Fort Regent; they were given to Conway in 1788 in gratitude for his service to the island.

REMENHAM

A SPARE SPIRE

Access: From Reading, take A4 east for 5½ miles to A321 roundabout. Turn left
towards Henley. Go 3 miles to junction with A4130, turn right towards
Marlow. Go ¾ mile. Opposite pub, take track ¼ mile to Park Place
Farm. Steeple can be seen on the right. NB: It stands on private land.

Map reference: Sheet 175 SU780823

The thirty-foot octagonal-section flèche of a Christopher Wren steeple in this quiet
meadow came from St Bride's Church, Fleet Street in London. This was one of the
"handsome spires rising in good proportion above the neighbouring houses".
Superseded, it was erected here to mark the accession of Queen Victoria in 1837 -
but its location gives it every appearance of being a folly.

SHOTTESBROOKE

A MYSTERIOUS KEY

DURING REPAIRS IN 1967 THIS KEY WAS FOUND INSIDE THE TOMB BELOW

Against the north wall of the chancel of St John Baptist, an effigy of William Throckmorton, Doctor of Laws, lies below a case containing a key. The priest was buried in 1535 with this key and the knowledge of what it unlocked.

Unusually, the Saxon holder of this manor was allowed to keep it after the Norman Conquest. He was Aelfward, the goldsmith charged with the task of preparing the crown at coronations. Presumably he produced that needed by King William I on Christmas Day 1066. Aelfward's father had held the land from Queen Edith, daughter of Earl Godwin of Wessex.

In 1337 Sir William Trussell formed a college here but the magnificent church is all that remains of it.

WOKINGHAM

BOUNDARIES

> *Access:* From Reading take A329 6¹/₂ miles to Broad Street. Before Town Hall, turn left into (one-way) Rose Street and park. Marker is on NW corner Rose Street and Wiltshire Road.
>
> *Map reference:*   Sheet 175 SU815088

The marker indicates a boundary between Berkshire and Wiltshire. Land nearby which belonged to the Lord of the Manor of Amesbury - the Earl of Salisbury - was deemed to be an enclave of Wiltshire. For similar reasons, Hurst was in Wiltshire and Oxenwood (Wiltshire - SU3059) was once in Berkshire. The boundaries were tidied in 1844 but this marker remained.

By comparison, the boundary revision of 1974 which stripped The Royal County of Berkshire of the Vale of Uffington and the White Horse seems bureaucratic nonsense.

CALIFORNIA

NAMES OLD AND NEW

California (SU797644) - like Egypt (SU443766) and Scotland (SU563694) - is a nickname; naming a settlement after a remote place is not uncommon. "Where's this, my fine fellow?" an Ordnance Survey officer might have asked in 1830. "Why, this be Egypt," he might have been told - so Egypt appears on the First Edition maps and a present-day sewage pump.

Berkshire's name probably comes either from the Celtic *barroc* - 'hilly' - or *bearru* - 'a wood'. River names are among the oldest: 'Thames' (British: *tamesa* - 'dark river' - cf Sanskrit: *tamasa*), 'Kennet' (Celtic: *cynetan* - 'to rise up' ie 'flood' - cf Welsh: *cynu* or *kuno* - 'exalted' ie 'worshipped'), 'Loddon' (British: *luta* - 'mud' - cf Gaelic: *lon* - 'a marsh'). Many places are named after Saxon people: 'Bracknell' (Old English *Bracca halh* - 'Bracca's corner of land'), 'Wokingham' (from Wocca's people's hamlet). Others describe the land: 'Remenham' (from *rimma* - 'a riverbank'), 'Twyford' (two fords), 'Winnersh' (from *wynn* - 'a meadow' - and *ersc* - 'ploughland' - ie, a bit of each), 'Speen' ('Spone' in 1086, from *spon* - 'woodchips'). In Reading, Orts Road takes its name from the monks' practice of giving leftover food (orts) to the poor; Forbury comes from *forburh* - 'land in front of a town entrance'. Aldermaston's tiny green, 'The Loosey' possibly got its name from either *hlose* - 'a pigsty' - or the Old English *lus* - 'louse-ridden cattle'.

FINCHAMPSTEAD

A GIANT AMONG TREES

Access:	From Reading head for Basingstoke. At A33/A327 roundabout go left on A327 5¼ miles to Arborfield Cross, continue on A327 for 3½ miles to T-junction with B3348. Turn left. Go 2¾ miles through village to NT car park.
Map reference:	Sheet 175 SU811634

Sequoiadendron Giganteum, the world's largest living thing, was discovered in the Sierra Nevada, California in 1852 - the year in which Wellington, the Iron Duke, died. The tree, named Wellingtonia in his honour, can reach 80 feet in girth and live for thousands of years. The B3348 towards Wellington College - which was opened as a national memorial to the Iron Duke in 1859 - is a ³/₄ mile avenue of 110 Wellingtonia trees. They were planted by the proprietor of *The Times,* John Walter III, in 1869 when every landowner in Britain was keen to have such exotic specimens on his estate. There was opposition to these "worthless" Californian trees from late Victorian gardeners such as William Robinson but, it has to be said, they form a spectacular memorial to Wellington - the man whose *Times* obituary described as having "exhausted nature and exhausted glory".

NINE MILE RIDE

A WAY-OUT PUB

Access:	From Reading head for Basingstoke. At A33/A327 roundabout go left on A327 5¼ miles to Arborfield Cross, bear left on B3349 towards Wokingham. After 1 mile, turn right at The Bull. After Barkham Square, bear left. After 1 mile, cross B3016. After ¼ mile bear left onto Nine Mile Ride. Go towards Crowthorne for 1½ miles, look on left for pub sign.
Map reference:	Sheet 175 SU824654

This remote pub is said to have got its name from a surprised Duke of Wellington who came across it while hunting. A space-age interpretation of the pub's name is depicted on the inn sign. Originally, the pub was a drinking place for squatters in Windsor Forest who scratched a livelihood by making besoms.

SANDHURST

UP THE STEPS

Access:	From Reading head for Basingstoke. At A33/A327 roundabout go left on A327 10 miles to A30. Go left 5 miles to Camberley. Guarded gates are on the left. NB: Access may be restricted.
Map reference:	Sheet 175 SU859608

© Jim Farrar

Old College at the Royal Military Academy Sandhurst was built between 1807 and 1812 at the height of the Napoleonic Wars. Its heroic size and severe design is dominated by the Grand Entrance, a Greek Revival Doric portico - an early use of the style in England. A broad flight of steps leads to a hall; into this, cadets to be commissioned as officers after the Sovereign's Parade must march. They are followed up the steps by the Adjutant on his horse.

Beneath the majestic portico is a barred cell used to house any cadet whose misconduct on parade justifies the ignominy of being marched at the double up those same steps. Here, it is said, the sunlight comes in stripes.

© Graham Buchanan-Dunlop

ARBORFIELD

CROPS, GENERALS & BOOTS, DICTATORS

Access:	From Reading head for Basingstoke. At A33/A327 roundabout go left on A327 5¼ miles to Arborfield Cross. Go on for ½ mile, turn left to Arborfield Garrison, turn right and follow signs to REME Museum.
Map reference:	Sheet 175 SU771658

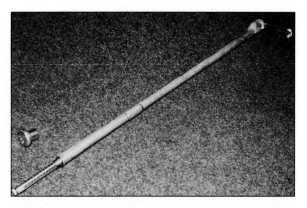

Major General Bertie Rowcroft's riding crop has a built-in tyre pressure gauge, handy when the horse power is wheeled. General Rowcroft, commissioned in 1911 into the Army Service Corps - which relied on the equine form - became the Father of the Corps of Royal Electrical and Mechanical Engineers (REME). An energetic organiser, he built a force of 160,000 men in seven months. It was put to the test only three weeks after REME's official formation: at the Battle of Alamein in October 1942.

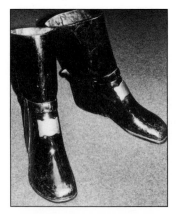

Il Duce's boots came from an equestrian statue which once overlooked the port of Tripoli in Libya. After the port was captured by the 8th Army on 23 January 1943, the bulky statue was broken up by REME for its valuable metal content. The boots, however, were kept as a souvenir by the officers' mess. It is rumoured that Mussolini's head found its way to South Africa.

The REME Museum is famous for its exquisitely made models of military vehicles and battle scenes - as befits an organisation which prides itself on craftsmanship.

STRATFIELD MORTIMER

A SAXON EPITAPH

Access: From Reading take A33 towards Basingstoke for 3¹/₂ miles, past M4 J11. Turn right at roundabout towards Mortimer. After 4 miles and past turning on left to the station, turn left to St Marys Church.

Map reference: Sheet 175 SU668641

The tomb slab in the south wall of the chancel is of Purbeck Marble, a good quality limestone. Around its border is a latin inscription. In the time of King Athelstan (reigned 924-39) efforts were made to improve the lapsed standard of latin scholarship. Later that century, Abbot Aelfric became known for his latin works; his patron was a thane named Aethelward who descended from King Alfred's brother. Aethelward wrote a chronicle which has been dated to around 1010. The inscription has been translated: "On 8th before Kalends of October Aegelward (sic) son of Kypping was laid in this place. Blessed be he who prays for his soul. Toki wrote this." Kypping was the thane who held the manor in the 10th century. The spelling of the name Aethelward could have been corrupted by the use of the Old English letter 'thorn' (whose capital resembles a 'P') in place of a latin 'TH'. However, there is mention in the Anglo-Saxon Chronicle of a thane named Aegelwardus who died in 1017. Put together, the clues indicate that the tomb slab could be his. As for Toki: his was a very common Scandinavian name.

The village takes the first part of its name from the latin. The Devil's Highway, the Roman street linking the British tribal town of Calleva Atrebatum (SU6462) with London, passes within a mile of the church.

SULHAMPSTEAD

HOME AND GARDEN

> *Access:*   From Reading take A4 4 miles west to M4 J12 and on 2 miles to left
> turn into village. House is on right opposite lane to Police College. NB:
> Garden (only) is open occasionally under National Gardens Scheme.
>
> *Map reference:*   Sheet 175 SU632686

Folly Farm is a beautiful example of the collaboration between an industrious
young architect and a middle-aged lady horticulturalist. Edwin Lutyens (1869-1944)
was already well regarded when, in 1906, he was commissioned to extend the
centuries-old farmhouse. A second extension was begun in 1912. Getrude Jekyll
(1843-1932), who had trained as a painter, designed over 300 gardens for Lutyens'
buildings. She loved water gardens in the Moorish tradition and the melding of
garden architecture with plantings. Lutyens' creative use of local brick, tile and
green oak is especially effective here: the roof seems to flow over the house like
pastry.

UFTON NERVET

A SAFE HOUSE

Access: From Reading take A4 west 4 miles to M4 J12 and on 3 miles to left turn to Ufton. After ³/₄ mile bear right for 1 mile to Ufton Court on right. NB: Open first Sunday in May only.

Map reference: Sheet 175 SU626667

The oak-framed Grade I listed Elizabethan manor house conceals traces of a medieval cruck-constructed hall. Francis Perkins, son of William Perkins of Brimpton inherited Ufton Court shortly after it was built in 1576. The Catholic link was strengthened when he married the daughter of Queen Mary I's ablest lawyer, Edmund Plowden. After the Babington Plot of 1586 brought suppression of Catholicism, Ufton became a safe house for priests. One wing (above) housed a chapel with a confessional (or oratory) and incumbents' lodgings; at least four secret priest holes were built. Wall decoration includes the dead Queen Mary's cipher and Tudor rose (right).

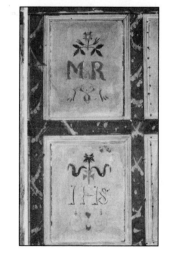

Spies reported Perkins' actions but no priest was caught; the chapel was raided in 1599 and a large hoard of treasure confiscated - but Perkins proved legal title. Considering the number of recusants who were bankrupted, tortured or executed at the time, the survival of Perkins and his safe house seems miraculous.

ALDERMASTON

CANDLE AUCTION

Access:	From Reading take A4 west 4 miles to M4 J12 and on 4 miles. Turn left onto A340 (Tadley). Go 2 miles to village. Go through village for 200 yards, turn left, and go 600 yards to St Mary the Virgin church on the right.
Map reference:	Sheet 174 SU597649

© R.B. Miller

Much of the village's common land was enclosed in 1801 and the vicar was granted the right to rent out a two-acre pasture for the benefit of his church. Every three years, in mid-December, an auction is held according to an ancient custom - thought to be French - similar to that described in Pepys diary entry for 3 September 1662. A pig's fat candle, pierced by a horseshoe nail an inch below the wick, is lit by the vicar who starts the bidding. The highest bidder at the time the flame reaches the nail gains the use of Church Acre for three years. Such auctions were legalised in the reign of King George III. In 1801 £7 was bid; by 1824 the church had acquired a new organ. Aldermaston is thought to be the last English village to hold such an auction. One took place on 19 December 1995.

ALDERMASTON

LOCK UP

Access:	From Reading take A4 west 4 miles to M4 J12 and on 4 miles. Turn left onto A340 (Tadley). Go 2 miles to village. The Hinds Head is on the right.
Map reference:	Sheet 174 SU590653

In the late 18th century, many villages had tiny prisons for use by the local constable. Without windows or heating, with an earth closet and straw for bedding they formed a "dull, dark dock" likely to deter petty criminals. They were also used as overnight accommodation for prisoners on their way to court or public execution.

Aldermaston's lock-up stands behind The Hinds Head whose landlord makes it known to today's unruly that he holds the key.

In Pangbourne, the lock-up is in the garden of Church Cottage (SU634764), a private house which from 1912 was the retirement home of Kenneth Grahame author of *The Wind in the Willows*. The book was inspired - not by this stretch of the Thames - but by that below Winter Hill near Cookham Dean.

NEWBURY

BEAKER FOLK

Access:	In Newbury District Museum in The Wharf.
Map reference:	Sheet 174 SU472671

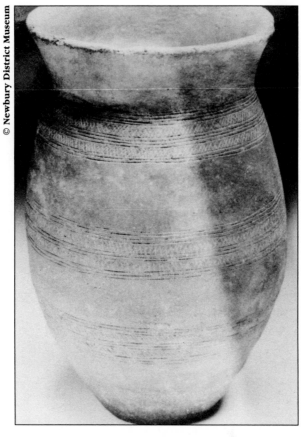

© Newbury District Museum

One of best preserved beakers of the early bronze age Beaker Folk was found at Inkpen. Hand formed - not wheel thrown - and bearing characteristic fine- toothed impressed decor, the 11-inches tall artifact dates from before 1600BC. The makers - named after the drinking cups they placed in graves with their dead - came from the Middle Rhine area of Central Europe. They moved to southern Britain in their quest for copper and tin with which they made spearheads and arrow tips.

NEWBURY

THROCKMORTON'S COAT

Access: In Newbury District Museum on The Wharf.

Map reference: Sheet 174 SU472671

In 1811, Sir John Throckmorton bet the Newbury clothier George Coxeter 1000 guineas that he couldn't turn the wool still on the backs of sheep in the morning into a coat to be worn at dinner on the same day. On 25 June at Greenham, two sheep were sheared, the wool carded, spun and wound onto a loom. Three and a half yards of cloth was woven, milled and teazed. The dyed cloth was sheared, pressed and tailored all within 13 hours and 20 minutes - in time for Sir John to wear his new coat at dinner time. Coxeter's success is authenticated by the original certificate displayed in the museum.

In September 1991 the feat was repeated by the Camp Hopson department store but 40 minutes quicker: the illustration is of the resulting coat. Throckmorton's Coat is to be seen at his family home: Coughton Court in Warwickshire (NT).

SHAW

A NEAR MISS

Access:	From Newbury, take B4009 (Shaw road) for 500 yards. Turn left into Church Road. Go 400 yards, Shaw House is on right. NB: The house is in the grounds of a school and not open to the public.
Map reference:	Sheet 174 SU488676

During the English Civil War, this was the home of Humphrey Dolman, a staunch Royalist. His battlecry was "King and Law, shouts Dolman of Shaw!" In October 1644, the house was defended by ramparts and cannon against the forces of Edward Montagu, Earl of

Manchester. King Charles I, who spent much of his time with his troops, was in an upper room in the south-east corner when it came under fire by a sniper. A bullet which narrowly missed the king pierced the panelling behind him. Above is a king's-eye view of the scene (left) and the sniper's view (right).

Shaw House, a Grade I listed building, was built in 1581 for a wealthy clothier, Thomas Dolman who countered criticism of his 'extravagance' by having a Greek motto inscribed over the door (left): *Let no jealous man enter.*

WASH COMMON

FALKLAND'S MEMORIAL

Access:　　In Newbury, from the Ring Road take A343 towards Andover for 1¹/₂ miles to junction with Essex Street. Memorial is on right. (NT)

Map reference:　　Sheet 174 SU459649

Of romantic stories of the English Civil War, that of Lucius Cary, Viscount Falkland (1610-1643) may dominate. Gentle, liberal intellectual Falkland was happier among theologians, philosophers and poets than at the court of King Charles I. But his father had been a soldier and statesman; Lucius was encouraged to follow his example. Today, the young man might be a champion of refugees; in 1640, he entered politics as a supporter of the Popular Party. A man of utter integrity, he was appointed a Privy Councillor and a Secretary of State. He worked hard to avoid civil war but when it came he took up arms, convinced of the King's cause. He plunged into the thick of the fighting urging his superiors to give

Cromwell's forces no respite and thus finish the violence quickly. But the war dragged on. At Newbury on 20 September 1643, depressed by seeing his intellectual friends killed one after another, he placed himself in the front rank of a cavalry regiment which faced murderous fire. Before the commander could widen the gap through which they must charge, Falkland spurred his horse forward and was killed instantly. Some say he was impetuous by nature, others point to the brutal end of his harmonious world and claim that he committed suicide.

CHIEVELEY

AN ABANDONED MASCOT

Access: From Newbury take Oxford Road (B4494) towards Wantage for 4½ miles to The Blue Boar Inn on the right.

Map reference: Sheet 174 SU455742

Lord Ingilby of Ripley Castle, Yorkshire, much taken by two Grecian sculptures of wild boars in the Uffizi Palace in Florence, had an Italian sculptor make copies. On 2 July 1644, Cromwell's Roundheads defeated Prince Rupert's Cavaliers at the Battle of Marston Moor not far from Ripley. The victors took one of the two boars as a mascot. On ·26 October they camped near Chieveley before the Second Battle of Newbury. Lord Ingilby's boar was abandoned at the inn; its partner may be seen in Ripley.

WINTERBOURNE

HOP CASTLE

Access: From Newbury take Oxford Road (B4494) towards Wantage for 4¹/₂
miles. Just past The Blue Boar turn left onto by-way. Walk 300 yards,
turn left for ¹/₂ mile, turn right to Penclose Farm. Folly is best seen in
winter 200 yards on the right. NB: Private property.

Map reference: Sheet 174 SU447738

Remote and inaccessible, the folly was built as a lodge in 1765 for John Elwes who
kept foxhounds and became an MP in 1771. In sturdy brick and flint, it has two
storeys of octagonal central rooms with square ones leading off to give a roughly
cruciform ground plan. Interior walls are decorated with shell patterns. The central
rooms have an ogival tiled roof; the side wings have hop finials which give the
folly its name. There was a tunnel connecting it to Penclose Farm and possibly a
second leading to The Blue Boar. Elsewhere such tunnels gave secret access to
diversions which would not be approved by the owner's wife.

LECKHAMPSTEAD

A FITTING MEMORIAL

Access: From Newbury take Oxford Road (B4494) 6 miles towards Wantage. At Egypt, turn left to Leckhampstead, go 500 yards to village green.

Map reference: Sheet 174 SU439764

The war memorial obelisk on the village green bears a clock with hands made of bayonets and roman numerals formed from rifle ammunition. The minutes are marked by machine gun bullets. Around the obelisk base is a chain from a ship which fought for the Royal Navy's pyrrhic victory of Jutland on 1 June 1916 - a victory which cost 6907 British lives. The chain links naval gun shells which remind us of the dreadnoughts' armament - in 1916, the most powerful guns ever fired in anger.

Although HMS Collingwood of the First Battle Squadron at Jutland survived almost unscathed, 21-year old Sub-Lieutenant Johnson of A turret came close to death when a salvo straddled the ship. Johnson's real name was Prince Albert, the future King George VI.

WEST ILSLEY

BORDER COUNTRY

Access:	From Newbury take A34 north 11 miles to slip road for West Ilsley. Go 2 miles to village and turn right for A34 and Chilton golf club. Go ½ mile up to Bury Down car park.
Map reference:	Sheet 174 SU478841

The Ridgeway was a major trading route of the bronze age Beaker Folk; it has been a footpath for 4000 years. The westward route (right) crosses what is now the Oxfordshire border to pass Scutchamer Knob. The name is from the Saxon *Cwichelmleah* - Cwichelm's clearing. On this high, defensible point the free men of neighbouring hundreds came to the Moot to deal with public business under the auspices of their reeve. To the east, the Ridgeway continues to the Thames which it crosses above Streatley. On this section is Roden Down (SU535820), the site of a 4th century Roman cemetery, and Lowbury Hill (SU540822) famous for the quantity of oyster shells discarded by the Romans. Under the scarp runs a section of Grim's Ditch (below) a bronze age earthwork used by the Saxons of the 6th century as a defence against their rivals in the Thames Valley. They gave it a nickname of Woden - *Grim*, the masked one - because they thought only a god could construct such a ditch.

The springy turf of the Downs above West and East Ilsley has been used for over two centuries for racehorse training; Prince William, Duke of Cumberland (1721-65) had stables here. But the most numerous passers-by are long gone: at one time, 400,000 sheep a year were sold at East Ilsley's fair under a charter granted by King James I.

HAMPSTEAD NORREYS

BERKSHIRE'S RAINFOREST

Access: From Newbury go north on A34 3 miles to M4 J13 then on ¹/₂ mile to
Chieveley slip road. Follow brown signs 5¹/₂ to Wyld Court.

Map reference: Sheet 174 SU543762

Wyld Court Rainforest is a conservation and education project for rainforest species
both plant and animal. The atmosphere within extensive glasshouses is
computer-controlled to replicate climatic Cloudforest, Amazonica and Lowland
Tropical conditions - the last at a very humid minimum of 21°C. The finest
collection of rainforest plants in England (begun by Barrie Findon in 1960) shares
these conditions with many of the insect, fish, reptile, bird and small mammal
species which balance the natural ecosystem. Rare plants, threatened by
unprecedented land clearance, have been propagated; endangered mammals, such
as Emperor Tamarins, breed happily here. Amongst the fifty rarest plants, is
Anthurium Warocqueanum (above left) from the lowland of tropical Colombia; it
is over sixty years old and probably extinct in the wild but is now a source of new
stock. Strangest of all is (above right) the purple and black Bat Flower - *Tacca
Chantrieri* from Amazonia - whose long whiskers are probably unique in the plant
world.

HAMPSTEAD NORREYS

A PYRAMID

Access:	From Newbury go north on A34 3 miles to M4 J13 then on ¹/₂ mile to Chieveley slip road. Right to Hermitage, left at B4009 3 miles to Hampstead Norreys, at T-junction, right 100 yards to St Mary's Church on right. Walk to south side.
Map reference:	Sheet 174 SU529763

Before he died in July 1855, Job Lowsley voiced a wish to be buried in a triangular piece of his land; as it was unconsecrated, permission was refused. But Job got his triangle: in 1876 the ironfounders N.Hedges of Bucklebury constructed a step pyramid above Job's grave.

In 1888, his son issued a glossary of Berkshire dialect words which supplemented Job's glossary of 1852. "Lark o'massy", as he might say.

The village was owned by the Norreys family who were prominent from the 13th until the 16th centuries. Henry Norreys, once gentleman-in-waiting to King Henry VIII and recipient of many favours, was executed in 1536 for alleged adultery with Anne Boleyn, mother of Queen Elizabeth I.

ALDWORTH

GIANTS

Access:	From Newbury go north 3 miles on A34 to M4 J13 and on ½ mile to Chieveley slip road. Right to Hermitage, left at B4009 3 miles to Hampstead Norreys. Follow B4009 to Aldworth 3½ miles. Left to village, St Mary's Church is on left.
Map reference:	Sheet 174 SU554795

The nave is dominated by nine enormous recumbent effigies of members of the 14th century de la Beche family. Sir Philip - reputed to be a giant - whose grandfather was knighted by King Edward I in 1278, was sheriff of the county in 1313-1314 and valet to the murdered King Edward II. Jailed as a rebel in 1322 after the defeat of Thomas Earl of Lancaster, he was pardoned by King Edward III. Another, Sir Nicholas, supervised the education of King Richard II's father, the Black Prince, and was entrusted with raising money for the war in France. He was sent to the Tower in 1340 by a furious King Edward III after the money was delayed. Legend has it that a tenth knight is buried beneath the church wall because he made a pact with the devil.

A memorial to the poet Lawrence Binyon (1869-1943) lies beside the churchyard's north boundary hedge. His words are heard on Remembrance Day:

> *"They shall not grow old as we that are left grow old ..."*

ALDWORTH

A PACKMAN'S PUB

Access: From Newbury go north on A34 3 miles to M4 J13 and on ¹/₂ mile to Chieveley slip road. Right to Hermitage, left at B4009 3 miles to Hampstead Norreys. Follow B4009 to Aldworth 3¹/₂ miles. Left past the church to village and The Bell Inn.

Map reference: Sheet 174 SU555796

Built around 1340, this cruck-constructed building became an inn which served packmen who travelled the Ridgeway in Tudor times. One - a tea dealer named James McQuhae - married the landlord's daughter and founded the family which still owns the inn.

In the 1860s, typhus in nearby Hungerford Green led the Inspector of Nuisances to recommend that the villagers should dig a new well. But the money provided was allocated by the vicar to church renovation. The villagers sent the vicar to Coventry and, until the well was dug, held all meetings in The Bell. Drought in 1926 required the well to be deepened to 372 feet, making it one of the deepest in England. When mains water came to Aldworth in 1937, the landlord of The Bell had the honour of drawing the last bucket from the well.

ASHAMPSTEAD
WALL PAINTINGS

Access: From Newbury go north on A34 3 miles to M4 J13 and on ¹/₂ mile to Chieveley slip road. Right to Hermitage, left at B4009 3 miles to Hampstead Norreys. Follow B4009 2 miles to Haw Farm, turn right, go a mile to Ashampstead. Turn right at crossroad for St Clements Church.

Map reference: Sheet 174 SU564768

The early 13th century paintings were discovered in 1895. Considered among the most important of their age in England, they include a Last Judgement over the chancel beam complete with a red devil.

The Earls of Warwick were the feudal overlords of the manor. In Reading's St Laurence Church, on the NW column of the western archway beneath the tower, is a graffito bear with a ragged staff - the symbol of the Warwicks.

ASHAMPSTEAD

AN ORATOR'S FOLLY

© Andrew Plumridge

In the mid-19th century, among many fervent religious sects the Primitive Methodists strove to gain a flock. They met hostility often - especially the female preachers. Isaac Septimus Nullis (1828-68), a tea dealer and insurance agent, was an enthusiastic evangelist. To practise his oratory, he built a pulpit in the form of a brick tower in his garden. Perhaps his favourite text was from Isaiah 42 v11: "Let them shout from the top of the mountains" - the house was later named Blorenge which is a mountain near Abergavenny in Wales. (OS Sheet 161 SO2712).

FRILSHAM

CIRCULAR CHURCHYARD

Access:	From Newbury, go north 4 miles on A34 to Chieveley slip road, right to Hermitage. At B4009, go left ¼ mile, bear right towards Bucklebury for ¾ mile, bear left to Frilsham. At crossroad, left to church.
Map reference:	Sheet 174 SU537732

Circular yards like St Frideswide's are rare and are believed to indicate pre-Christian origin of the place of worship. It is unlikely that the yard would have been a pagan cemetery: such burial grounds were set apart from temples and villages. Perhaps the circle was taken over by early Christians because - for a defined area - its perimeter presents the shortest line to defend against the forces of evil. The iron railings by Hedges of Bucklebury have served that purpose since the reign of King George IV.

St Frideswide was the daughter of a Mercian prince. After fleeing to Oxford to avoid a forced marriage, she founded a priory which was suppressed in 1525. Its church became Oxford's cathedral; its monastic buildings, converted by Wolsey into Cardinal's College, were renamed King Henry VIII's College and then, in 1546, Christ Church. St Frideswild, who died in 735AD, is the patron saint of Oxford University.

STANFORD DINGLEY

GOOD GAME

Access: From Newbury, take A4 east for 3 miles through Thatcham. Turn left for Upper Bucklebury. Go 1¼ miles to T-junction, turn right. Go 2½ miles to Chapel Row. Turn left towards Bucklebury. After ¼ mile, turn right to Stanford Dingley. At T-junction go left 300 yards to pub on right.

Map reference: Sheet 174 SU576716

In the tap room of the 16th century Bull Inn, the game of 'Ring the bull' has been played for at least two centuries. A hook representing a bull's nose is set in the wall below a bull's horns; a five-foot length of cord attached to the ceiling five feet from the hook has a nose-ring on its free end. The idea is to swing the ring onto the hook. Each player is allowed 20 attempts - the player with the highest number of successful attempts wins; a player who scores 20 may claim a bottle of whisky.

BUCKLEBURY

MEMENTO MORI

Access: From Newbury go north on A34 3 miles to M4 J13 then on ¹/₂ mile to Chieveley slip road. Right to Hermitage. At B4009 turn left, go ¹/₄ mile, bear right to Bucklebury 3¹/₂ miles. St Mary's Church on left. NB: Permission to see the ringing chamber is needed.

Map reference: Sheet 174 SU553708

In this village, the Hedges family worked an iron foundry for years. As a result, the churchyard - like those of nearby villages - contains many cast iron memorials. It seems that these intimations of mortality got to Nathaniel Hedges who, in 1771, inscribed his own epitaph into a window pane in the ringing chamber of the tower.

In the chancel is another reminder that time flies: a stained glass panel consisting of a sundial and a realistic housefly.

CHAPEL ROW

A MAMMOTH BONE

Access: From Newbury, take A4 east for 3 miles through Thatcham. Turn left for Upper Bucklebury. Go 1¹/₄ miles to T-junction, turn right. Go 2¹/₂ miles to junction with Woolhampton road. Pub is on right.

Map reference: Sheet 174 SU572697

Bladebone Inn's gold-painted copper sign encloses a mammoth scapular. The enormous bone was found buried in the flood plain of the River Kennet some time before 1666 when farthing tokens depicting it were issued here.

THATCHAM
BAILY'S BEADS

> *Access:* From Newbury take A4 3 miles towards Reading. In Thatcham turn right at Broadway-High Street sign, turn right into Church Gate. St Mary's Church is on right.
>
> *Map reference:* Sheet 174 SU516672

Francis Baily (1774-1844) explored the wilds of North America in 1796-98 before taking up a lucrative career on the Stock Exchange. Having published books on actuarial practice, he retired a rich man at the age of 51. But throughout he had a secondary interest - astronomy. He remodelled the Nautical Almanack, calculated the Earth's density and, in 1827, issued a revised catalogue of 2881 stars. When fire destroyed the 1758 Standard Yard measure, Baily produced the replacement. His name lives on in the term he gave to a phenomenon seen during a total solar eclipse: light passing through irregularities in the moon's horizon gives the impression that the disc is bordered by a ring of beads. Baily died while serving as president of the Royal Astronomical Society which he helped found in 1820. The tablet on the church's south wall commemorates his extraordinarily full life of three score years and ten.

By contrast, on the north wall is a memorial to Arthur Buller Turner, 2nd Royal Berkshire Regiment. On 28 September 1915 - almost single-handedly - he cleared a German position at Fosse during the Battle of Loos. He died of his wounds and was awarded the Victoria Cross. He was 22.

BRIMPTON

FARM CHAPEL

Access: From Newbury take A4 5 miles east through Thatcham to turning on right to Brimpton. Go 1½ miles. After chapel on left and bend to right look on right for Manor Farm.

Map reference: Sheet 174 SU558653

In the garden of the farmhouse is the flint chapel of St Leonard. Above the north door is a Maltese cross on a fish scale background. Built by the Knights Templar, the chapel would have a teaching function - which it retained after becoming a chantry in the 14th century. In 1547, the ten-year old puppet King Edward VI's Chantries Act abolished all 2374 chantries in England. But the tide turned: William Perkins, tenant here of Sir Francis Englefield, became gentleman usher to Cardinal Pole (1500-58) - great-nephew of King Edward IV - when Queen Mary I recalled him from 17 years' exile. But the tide turned again: Perkins's royal and Catholic connections brought him unwelcome attention when Queen Elizabeth I's life was threatened in 1586. His son Francis inherited Ufton Court in 1581.

HUNGERFORD

TUTTI FRUTTI

> *Access:*   On the Tuesday after Easter Week in the High Street.
>
> *Map reference:*   Sheet 174 SU339684

© Newbury Weekly News

Hocktide takes its name from the Anglo-Saxon *heah* - high; it falls a week after Easter. St Brice's Festival, celebrating the genocide of the Danes in 1002, was traditionally a time for collecting money for parish purposes - from men on Monday and from women on Tuesday. On the Friday of Easter week, the Constable convenes the Hocktide Court Leet; the portreeve (an office dating from the reign of King Alfred - 871-901AD) collects quit rents, the bailiff collects market dues and new businesses pay a levy. On the Tuesday, a 350-year old horn is blown by the Bellman as he tours the town warning commoners - who may graze two cows and a horse on the common - to attend the Court on pain of a penny fine. Two tuttimen (tithing-men) bearing poles tipped by nosegays go about the common-right houses distributing oranges in exchange for kisses in lieu of pennies from the ladies. 'Tutti', according to Lowsley's 1852 glossary of Berkshire dialect, means a bunch of flowers.

The lord of the manor in this most democratic of towns was once Simon de Montford who displaced the ineffectual King Henry III and, in 1265, formed the first English parliament.

HUNGERFORD
A DELIGHTFUL BRIDGE

Access:	On east side of Bridge Street beside canal bridge.
Map reference:	Sheet 174 SU338686

Nikolaus Pevsner in his architectural survey *The Buildings of England*, describes this unusual Regency house as "a delight". An iron footbridge links the front door on the first floor with the roadway. Beneath is a footpath allowing townspeople access to the canal which was opened in 1798.

A stranger feature centres a supermarket at 109 High Street: an 18th century manor house doorway.

HUNGERFORD

SWING BRIDGE

Access:	From High Street, walk down Church Street turn right to church. Follow path on left to canal.
Map reference:	Sheet 174 SU326685

The bridge of 1816 is a reminder of the importance of a canal which cut through ancient pathways and divided farmland - as new roads do today. A Kennet-Avon canal was proposed by Professor Briggs of Oxford University who surveyed a route in 1626. A section was built between Reading and Newbury in 1723 against violent opposition but the project was not practicable until the 'canal mania' of the 1790s overcame the objections of landowners and turnpike operators. In 1795 the section was enlarged to take 128-ton 'Newbury' barges. Above Newbury, a new stretch, designed by Rennie for 50-ton boats, opened to Hungerford in 1798. London and Bristol were linked by waterway in 1810, nearly two centuries after Briggs' proposal. For a few boom years the canal carried Kintbury whiting to the colourmen of Bristol, Somerset coal, Bath stone and Reading beer to London - and the products of Gibbons' iron works from Hungerford. The canal's decline began after the Great Western Railway linked London with Bristol in 1841; in 1847 a railway reached Hungerford. Canal receipts plumetted. By 1900 through traffic had ceased. Between 1848 and 1909 tonnage carried dropped by 85 per cent. Today, thanks to the work of the Kennet and Avon Canal Trust, the swing bridge is in frequent use.

AVINGTON

MEDIEVAL DEVILS

Access:	From Hungerford A338/A4 junction go east on A4 2 miles, turn right onto estate road. Church is at end of road on left. NB: Privately owned but access is allowed.
Map reference:	Sheet 174 SU372679

The medieval font of the Norman 12th century church of SS Mark and Luke is decorated with carvings of Princes of the Church, lawyers and clerks among whom prowls a devil. Is this whispering figure tempting Judas to betray Christ or does it warn god-parents of the baptised that, in the name of the child, they must renounce the devil and all his works? And are the grotesques (below) which grinned down from the chancel arch at the faithful of the middle ages another reminder of the proximity of evil?

The beakhead motif on the chancel arch was first used in England at Reading Abbey around 1125 (see page 29) and probably has a pagan origin. The ornamentation of arches and jambs with chevron and 'beaker' moulding produces alternations in light and shade which give an enhanced impression of solidarity in the stonework.

The south doorway of St Laurence Tidmarsh (see page 36) demonstrates a transition point: the chevrons there have 'eyes'.

KINTBURY

WINTERBOURN'S LOCAL

Access: From Hungerford, take A4 east for 3 miles. At crossroads, turn right to
Kintbury. Follow road through village back towards Hungerford. Pub
is on right.

Map reference: Sheet 174 SU381668

In 1830, rioting broke out against landlords who introduced farm machinery which put men out of work. The ringleaders based themselves at the Blue Ball Inn, a place well known for prize-fighting. Unfortunately, the authorities had disbanded the local militia two years before and had to call in the Grenadier Guards from London. Helped by former members of the Newbury Troop Berkshire Yeomanry Cavalry, the soldiers arrested 138 men. A special assizes in Reading convicted 70 and condemned 28 to death. Horrified local people petitioned. Sentences were commuted to transportation for all but three ringleaders. Two were reprieved at the last minute but William Winterbourn was hanged outside Reading Gaol on 17 January 1831. The rest were sent to the hulks until setting sail on the *Eliza* for New South Wales and the *Eleanor* for Tasmania. Most chose not to return to England.

INKPEN

CROCUSES

Access:	From High St Hungerford, take Park St onto the common. Bear right, go 3 miles to Inkpen Lower Green. At oblique T-junction, bear right. After 50 yards turn left towards Combe, go 200 yards to crossroad, turn left ½ mile to Upper Green, bear left. After 700 yards look left for narrow concrete lane (Pottery Road) before reaching playing field. Walk 200 yards up Pottery Road, entrance to crocus field is on the left. NB: The reserve is managed by BBONT.
Map reference:	Sheet 174 SU370645

The thousands of *crocus vernus* here (see back cover) represent the largest population of wild crocuses in Britain. The plant is not a native but is known to have flourished here since 1800. The variety is the parent of numerous varieties of modern Dutch crocuses. It is possible that corms were brought from their Southern European mountain home by members of the Knights Hospitaller of St John who served a nearby almshouse. The purple and white-purple flowers are to be seen in March.

INKPEN

A LONELY DEATH

Access: From High St Hungerford, take Park St onto the common. Bear right,
go 3 miles to Inkpen Lower Green. At oblique T-junction go left past
the Swan Inn and on for 1¹/₄ miles to a T-junction. Walk left towards
Kintbury. From the Inkpen sign on the right side of the road, go 33
paces and look right through laurels at brick wall 3 paces from road.

Map reference: Sheet 174 SU376647

A cross cut into a brick garden wall marks the spot where Thomas Bailey, a 67-year
old labourer, died of cold in The Great Snowstorm of 18 January 1881 within a
hundred yards of his home. After a strenuous day of threshing in Kintbury he had
fallen exhausted at about 7.30 pm. John Panting carried him to Inkpen but, when
Thomas said he could manage the final yards, left him and went to the pub.
Thomas was found dead at 9 pm by passers-by. The inquest heard how two young
men bullied Thomas at work: they were reprimanded by the coroner for their
cruelty.

The cross was almost forgotten but Mr Dowdell (born 1910), one-time gardener at
a nearby house, was able to point it out.

INKPEN HILL

COMBE GIBBET

Access:	From High St Hungerford, take Park St onto the common. Bear right, go 3 miles to Inkpen Lower Green. At oblique T-junction bear right 50 yards then turn left towards Combe, over crossroads and 1¼ miles up steep hill to summit. Turn right on by-road 400 yards to gibbet.
Map reference:	Sheet 174 SU364622

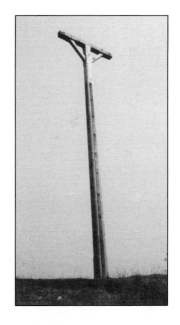

On the highest chalk hill in England, 975 feet above sea level, stands the latest of a series of gibbets. An earlier one displayed the corpses of George Broomham of Combe and Dorothy Newman of Inkpen who were hanged at Eastwick on 7 March 1676 for the murder of George's wife and son. In 1948, John Schlesinger, a twenty-two year old film director whose parents lived nearby, made a film of the story entitled *The Black Legend*.

Today, the hill is used for another form of aerial suspension - hang-gliding.

WALBURY CAMP

HARD TRAINING

Access:	From High St Hungerford, take Park St onto the common. Bear right, go 3 miles to Inkpen Lower Green. At oblique T-junction bear right 50 yards then turn left towards Combe, over crossroads and 1¹/₄ miles up steep hill to summit. Turn left to car park. Plaque is north of road.
Map reference:	Sheet 174 SU 371621

In 1944, the 9th Battalion of The Parachute Regiment commanded by Lt Col Terence BH Otway, trained on this steep hillside for the vital task of knocking out the Nazi's Merville Battery which dominated the eastern flank of Sword Beach in Normandy. Just after midnight on 6th June 1944, Otway dropped with 700 of his men but they were scattered widely. And the 100 Lancaster bombers which should have softened his target also missed their mark. Only 150 men gathered for the assault. Otway's orders made the vital nature of his mission clear: the guns must be destroyed before dawn and he must not contemplate failure. With no artillery support and only one heavy machine-gun, they fought a desperate hand to hand battle and won. The mighty guns were silenced at the cost of nearly half his men. Colonel Otway's bravery was marked by the award of the Distinguished Service Order. This plaque was erected to mark the place where he trained his men so effectively for battle.

WICKHAM
ELEPHANTS IN THE ROOF

Access: From M4 J14 go north on A34 ½ mile, right on B4000 2¼ miles to Wickham crossroad, right 300yds. Chapel is set back on left. *Map reference:*   Sheet 174 SU395715

St Swithun's chapel-at-ease was much restored in Victorian times. Strangely, the roof of the 1827 north aisle is supported by eight life-size papier-maché elephant heads. Four of them came from the Paris Exhibition of 1862 where they represented fortitude, docility, strength and reliance; the others are replicas. They make a change from angels.

The chapel's tower is Saxon - the oldest in the county. It was built as a watch tower on a Roman site possibly as early as the 7th century. The mullions of the north and south belfry windows are reused Roman balusters.

LAMBOURN
THE WAGES OF SIN

Access: From Hungerford take A338 towards Wantage. 1/2 mile after M4 J14, turn left onto B4000. Go 6 miles to Lambourn. Church is at junction with B4001. In churchyard, go to west door then north to railing and look west for stone.

Map reference: Sheet 174 SU326789

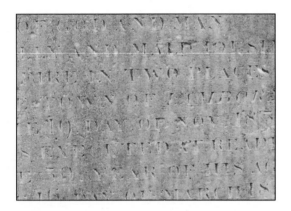

An epitaph on a tombstone close enough to the churchyard boundary to be read by passers-by, serves as a warning to the hot-headed. In late 1832, at a time when 'machine riots' and discontent over parliamentary reform were a major cause for concern among landowners, a farm labourer named John Carter demanded a rise; when it was refused, he got drunk and set fire to his employer's property. Egged on by friends, he raised more fires in the village. He was convicted of arson - a capital offence - and hanged on 16 March 1833 at Reading. Before he died he asked that he should be buried at this spot as a warning to others. His epitaph includes the words 'the wages of sin is death'.

In the 17th century a Mr Bush devised a 'ship' which could travel by air, land and water. Starting from Lambourn church tower - aided by ropes - the strange craft made its way to the Pool of London. Gouge marks on the tower record the event.

It is said that there are as many racehorses as people in Lambourn. They are best seen at Windsor, Ascot and Newbury.

UPPER LAMBOURN
VALLEY OF THE RACEHORSE

88

THE ROYAL COUNTY OF BERKSHIRE

A map showing some main roads
and page numbers indicating places of interest

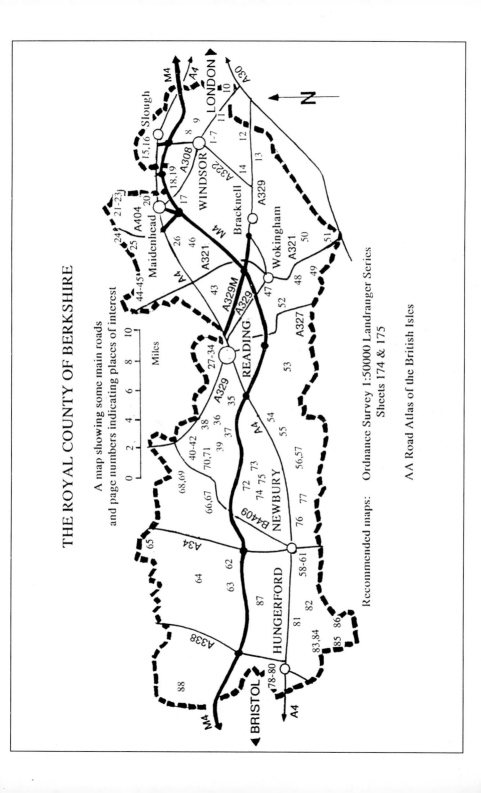

Miles

0 2 4 6 8 10

Recommended maps: Ordnance Survey 1:50000 Landranger Series
Sheets 174 & 175

AA Road Atlas of the British Isles

INDEX